Pretty Little

TRUTHS

MODERN DEVOTIONALS *for* YOUNG WOMEN

———

MANDY FENDER

ISBN 978-0-9822190-3-4

DEDICATION

For every young woman longing to be closer to Christ

Matthew 7:7 "Ask and it will be given unto you; seek and you will find; knock and the door will be opened to you."

TABLE OF CONTENTS

PRETTY LITTLE BONUS DEVOTIONALS

PRETTY LITTLE STUDY TIPS

WEEK 1

NO MORE DRAMA

'Drama'...the word that has plagued women everywhere since the beginning of time. All of the drama began with the very first woman with the first bite of the forbidden fruit.

Drama was never intended to be a part of real life. A drama is supposed to be a part of a written screen play and not a part of our lives. Unfortunately, it has crept its way into many of our lives. How do we avoid all the drama? Some drama may not be caused by you, but somehow you find yourself right smack dab in the middle of it. So how do you get out of it? The only answer to the drama is Jesus. He has made a way out of all the drama when we rely on Him and trust Him.

The best thing to do in the middle of drama is keep your mouth shut while removing yourself from the situation, if at all possible. As a believer, it is our responsibility and privilege to be peacemakers. Do everything on your part to not stir the pot of drama. Do your best to keep your hand out of the mess.

If there is no clear way out and you are stuck in the thick of it, PRAY! Really pray with all of your heart and give God control of the drama. Just because you are in the middle of it does not mean that you have to participate in it. Keep a cool head about you by filling your mind with scriptures. Keep calm by letting patience have her perfect work in you.

Romans 12:18 "If it is possible, as far as it depends on you, live at peace with everyone."

It is possible to keep the peace by controlling your actions and your words. Most of the drama in your life is dependent on one thing, and that is YOU. Loving drama is not of God. If you love drama, ask God to deliver you from it. There is a life of peace that starts on the inside of you and works its way throughout your life. Find peace in your heart and mind and you will find peace everywhere.

Pretty LittleCHALLENGE

This week, focus on living a peaceful, drama-free life.
It is possible!

WEEK 2

FILTERS

Have you ever seen a picture of someone and then you see them in real life and you think to yourself, *'Man, they look nothing like their picture?'* They might have had a crop, chop, and filter overload making them unrecognizable. Have you ever seen someone filter who they really were when certain people were around?

Some filters can be a good thing. For example, when we filter water that is a good thing. Even better, when we filter the words that come out of our mouth, that is a good thing. But when we start trying to hide who we really are it can become dangerous. We learn to hide and filter to make other people think we are something that we are not. Why? Sometimes we do it to be accepted while other times we do it to keep from getting in trouble. Learn how to show your true colors through Christ.

If you need help ask for help. Do your very best not to hide when you are in trouble. We cannot filter our troubles when it comes to God. God knows the secrets of our hearts, so there is no hiding it from Him in the first place. God is there to help you, not to condemn you. We will be known by the fruit that we produce.

Some will try to filter rotten fruit to make it look better. Do not be fooled. Look past the distracting filters and look at their real unfiltered fruit. Allow God to help you see

11

people's true colors. Let Him show you whether or not they are from Him. Live your life with no filters. Be unashamed of who you are in Christ. There is no need to hide any flaws behind filters because Jesus is now the only filter you need.

**Matthew 7:20 "By their fruit you
will recognize them."**

Will we be able to recognize you by your fruit?
Are you hiding behind any filters?
Will you allow Jesus to be the only filter you need?

_____

Pretty Little CHALLENGE

This week, focus on living without worldly filters and let Jesus be your filter.

WEEK 3

IT'S COMPLICATED

We have all probably said this in our lives at one point or another, especially when it comes to relationships. What do we really mean when we say *'It's complicated?'* Complicated means to have many connected parts which may cause confusion, or it can mean difficult to understand, or hard to explain. We have to really dig down deep and ask ourselves why we make things so complicated? Are they really that complicated? Or are we just frustrated and don't want to take the time to figure it out.

On-and-off again relationships are considered complicated, but in reality it is just two people who can't make up their minds. Complications may arise in this life that are out of our hands, and that is another story. If it is in our hands we do not need to make it more complicated than it has to be.

In this passage of scripture we see that life is too short and precious to make it all complicated unnecessarily.

1 Corinthians 7:29-31(Message) "I do want to point out, friends, that time is of the essence. There is no time to waste, so don't complicate your lives unnecessarily. Keep it simple—in marriage, grief, joy, whatever. Even in ordinary things—your daily routines of shopping, and so on. Deal as sparingly as possible with the things the world thrusts on you. This world as you see it is on its way out."

Of course, this world will thrust complications at you. It is the world, that is what it does. How you respond to the complications of this life is up to you. This world is on its way out, but the believer knows when the world goes out, Jesus steps in. Walk in faith and out of complications.

Pretty Little CHALLENGE

This week, focus on making your life less complicated according to the Word of God.

WEEK 4

TRUST ISSUES

Have you ever not known who you could trust? It is a terrible feeling not to know who is really on your side. It can be hard not knowing which friends really have your back. Trust is earned while respect should be freely given. You see, you can only trust those who have shown that they are trustworthy.

Trust is built on relationship; the stronger the relationship, the stronger the bond of trust. Hopefully most people have at least one person they can depend and count on. But even if there is no one on earth that we feel like we can trust there is the one and true living God who we can trust, beyond a shadow of a doubt. God is trustworthy because He has proven Himself to be so.

When God says 'yes', He means 'yes'. When He says 'no', He means 'no'. When He says He 'has you', then He 'has you'. God cannot lie. Everything He says is fact. You can count on it and you can believe it. If you have trouble trusting God, it is because you need to build your relationship with Him. That relationship that you build will keep you trusting Him even in the most difficult of circumstances. Trust God with all of your heart and lean not to your own understanding.

The bottom line in our lives has to be that we trust God no matter what. We have to know that if He says it, there is a reason for it and a reward in it. Trust will make you obey. Trusting in God will make you a better person.

Psalm 62:8 "Trust in him at all times, you people; pour out your hearts to him, for God is our refuge."

The Word does not tell us to only trust Him in the good times or the bad times, but at ALL TIMES. When you don't understand, trust God. When you do not know why, trust God. When you do not know how, trust God. Give God the honor by trusting Him. Build your relationship with God so that your trust in Him can begin to grow.

This week, focus on trusting God like you never have before and watch your life become more blessed than ever before.

WEEK 5

GROUNDED

The words every teenager dreads to hear: *'You are grounded.'* Grounded is usually a form of punishment, but in this devotional let us look at it as motivation to get deeply rooted in Christ. Let us look at the word 'grounded' as another way to say rooted, level-headed, and humble.

If someone calls you 'down to earth', it is meant as a compliment. It means you remember where you came from. We must learn this practice in our everyday lives. We must learn to be grounded and remember where we came from. We came from God, so it is important that we live like it.

Prideful and arrogant people need to look at what they are rooted in. Most of the time you will see those that are prideful are heavily rooted in themselves and those that are arrogant are rooted in their abilities. We have to come to the realization that we need to humble our flesh and be rooted in Christ.

Pride comes before the fall, so let us remove the pride we have in ourselves and become proud of something greater. Let the pride we have be for our Lord and Savior, Jesus Christ, because without Him, we would not be here. Without Him I realize I am nothing. It is when we are grounded in Him that we become who He wants us to be.

God wants us rooted in love and level-headed in every situation.

Colossians 2:6-7 "So then, just as you received Christ Jesus as Lord, continue to live your lives in him, rooted and built up in him, strengthened in the faith as you were taught, and overflowing with thankfulness."

Just like when our earthly parents ground us and take away things that distract us, we need to remove the distractions and ground ourselves in Christ so that we can grow. Be thankful for the opportunity to be grounded.

Pretty Little CHALLENGE

This week, focus on being grounded in Him.

WEEK 6

GUYS AND ROSES

When you are a teenage girl, there is not much sweeter than a cute boy with roses. When he hopefully knocks on the door (not honks at you from the car) with a hand full of flowers, your heart can feel like it's melting. Some old sayings would say, *'You are like putty in his hands.'*

WAIT, STOP, HOLD UP! I know that they are cute and all, and some may very well be quite sweet, but please let your heart only be putty in the hands of God. If you are changing who you are in Christ for anyone or anything, it is wrong. If a young man makes you want to change your morals and convictions and if he turns them against what God says, RUN. That's right, RUN. Run for your spiritual life.

If you go against what you have believed your whole life for the pleasure of one moment, understand that there is forgiveness that can cover up anything. But also use that moment to learn and grow from. Don't allow yourself in situations where you would have to question whether or not you can live up to your morals. Give the devil no place. If you know that you are attracted to a certain someone, don't be alone with them. Hormones run wild and sometimes they will try to get the best of you.

Submit your will to the will of God and not to a boy. It is true what they say; if he loves you, he will wait. Resist the urges that all teenagers get. It might not be popular to resist, but resisting sin means that the devil will flee from you. Remember, it is because God loves you that He sets up boundaries to protect you.

**James 4:7 "Submit yourselves, then, to God.
Resist the devil, and he will flee from you."**

Women of all ages have to resist temptations. Let God draw the line and then don't cross it. It will make adulthood so much easier when you learn boundaries. You always have two choices: you can submit to the flesh or submit to God. Submitting to God's will is so much more gratifying than submitting to anyone else's will, even our own. God is knocking at the door of your heart with a rose of love, forgiveness, and purpose.

Pretty Little CHALLENGE

This week, remember God's rose for you is forever and its
beauty never fades. Run from temptations and
run into the loving arms of your Father.

WEEK 7

IDENTITY CRISIS

There are a lot of people and things out there that would love to steal your identity. There are people who will try to tell you who you are, and there are things that would like to try to define you. Where is your identity found?

The world will try to identify you by how you look on the outside and how you feel on the inside. We have to stop being identified by looks and feelings and start to be identified by who we are in Christ. Our identity is found in Him. Our whole purpose of living is to be identified with Him.

If the world identifies people by what they see, would they see you are a Christian? Would they know by your actions who you really are? Before people come to Christ, they are confused about who they are. They search and search to try to find their true identities. It is not until they come to Christ that they truly find themselves.

We live in a world that is continually trying to find itself. We live in a culture where people are continually trying to reinvent themselves. If you are at a point in your life where you are trying to figure out who you really are, then you need to turn to Christ. When you seek Him you will find not only Him, but you will find yourself as well. You will find that the very breath on the inside of you is from Almighty God and that your identity is not found by any other way.

1 Peter 2:10 (NLT) "Once you had no identity as a people; now you are God's people. Once you received no mercy; now you have received God's mercy."

When you find the truth of who He is you can find the truth of who you are. There is so much more to you than outward appearance. There is even so much more to you than the way you feel.

Pretty Little CHALLENGE

This week, focus on who you are in Christ.

WEEK 8

RELATIONSHIP STATUS

What is your relationship status right now? Are you in one, out of one, or don't care to be in one? What about this question: What is your relationship status with God? Is your status with God good, bad, or ugly?

Every morning we wake up we should double check our relationship status with Him to make sure we are on the right track. We need to make sure that we are in agreement with His status toward us. Have we determined in our hearts that we will live according to His relationship rules? We have to be willing to listen to God's relationship advice.

If He tells us to cut ties in a certain relationship it is only to make our relationship with Him stronger. There are plenty of people who do not consider our relationship status with the Lord because either they don't know, they are against it, or they simply do not care.

We have to guard our relationship with the Lord and let nothing hinder it. If you have to break up with anyone, do not break up with God. His relationship with you is literally eternal. Let nothing come between you and the Lord. If you have to break off earthly relationships, so be it. Will it be painful? Yes, absolutely. Sometimes our hearts will hurt due to the letting go of other relationships. We must keep the most important relationship of all, at all costs. Our forever is not based on earthly relationships but our heavenly relationship with God, the Father.

2 John 1:9 (NLT) "Anyone who wanders away from this teaching has no relationship with God. But anyone who remains in the teaching of Christ has a relationship with both the Father and the Son."

Remain in the teaching of Christ. Remember what relationship is the most important. Remember who your true best friend is. Have a real conversation with Him, where you talk AND listen. When you have a real relationship with Him, you have real access to Him.

---

*Pretty Little*CHALLENGE

This week, learn to value your relationship with God and make Him the priority over all other relationships.

WEEK 9

FORGOTTEN BEAUTY

Everyone is so enamored with things of beauty. People want to go to beautiful places with beautiful people and have a beautiful time. There is nothing wrong with that, but we have forgotten what is truly beautiful.

We need to learn to see the beauty in every day and realize that life in itself is beautiful. Outward beauty is nice but it is that inner beauty that will radiate into all eternity. God is looking for young women whose hearts are beautiful. He is looking for the young women who are kind, generous, and show humility.

Search the beauty of your heart. Find all the good things about yourself and glorify God with them. Find all the parts of yourself that might not be so beautiful and give them to God. If you have anger, give it to God so He can give you beautiful patience. If you have hurt, give it to God so He can make it a beautiful testimony. Whatever you give to God is made beautiful.

Always remember God gives beauty for ashes and He has made everything beautiful in its time.

Trusting in our outward beauty to take us places will only end up disappointing us and eventually one day fail us. Trusting in the beauty of our salvation and allowing Jesus to make our hearts beautiful will stand the test of time.

1 Peter 3:3-4 "Your beauty should not come from outward adornment, such as elaborate hairstyles and the wearing of gold jewelry or fine clothes. Rather, it should be that of your inner self, the unfading beauty of a gentle and quiet spirit, which is of great worth in God's sight."

Take a look at your inner self. What do you see? God sees a chance to make a beautiful person even more beautiful by making her heart beautiful. Take the time on your inward appearance just like you take the time on your outward appearance.

Pretty Little CHALLENGE

This week, focus on your inner beauty
more than your outer beauty.

WEEK 10

FEARLESS

In this world there are so many things to fear. How can we possibly be fearless when there seems to be so many things to fear? Just watching the news can strike fear in the hearts of even the strongest of men.

How do we, as young women, become fearless?

Three words...HOPE, LOVE, and TRUST

We learn not to fear because we have a hope that even when things go terribly wrong, we have a Savior to help us get it right again. We have a love that pulls us out of the darkest of places. We have built a relationship of trust with the Maker of heaven and earth. We know that we do not have to fear when we give God control of the fear.

He told us to fear not. He told us to be strong and courageous. He told us that in this world we will have tribulations, but to be of good cheer because He has overcome this world.

We do not have to fear because everything we face has already been overcome. Overcome the fear with your hope, love, and trust. Understand God is greater. Let Him be greater than your fear. Let Him be greater than your circumstance.

2 Timothy 1:7 "For God hath not given us the spirit of fear; but of power, and of love, and of a sound mind."

Pretty Little CHALLENGE

This week, when fear tries to attach itself to you, remember this scripture and quote it in every situation you fear.

WEEK 11

POP QUIZ

The dreaded pop quiz! When you are at school and your teacher says, "Alright, put your books away; time for a pop quiz." It might make you a little uneasy because it was unexpected and unplanned.

The great thing about being a believer is that we get to have open book pop quizzes. God lets us see the answers when we read the Bible. Sometimes understanding the Word can be difficult. That is why it is so important to pray before you read so that way you can ask God to show you what He means.

We are responsible for rightly dividing God's Word in our hearts. Let God teach you and "tutor" you every single day of your life. In Psalm 26 we see that it is important to allow God to test our hearts to see where we are.

We must ask God to test us, try us, and examine our hearts and our minds. He will show you where you are, when you listen. He will give you instructions for everything. His lesson plans are loving and compassionate.

He will teach you how to react and respond to life. He will teach you when to speak and when to stay silent. He will teach you in every way imaginable if you let Him.

Allowing God to test your heart will help you when you examine your own heart. We must take an internal look at ourselves every day to see where we are in our faith.

2 Corinthians 13:5 "Examine yourselves to see whether you are in the faith; test yourselves. Do you not realize that Christ Jesus is in you--unless, of course, you fail the test?"

We don't want to fail the test of life, so how do we pass? We pass when we listen to the teacher and pay attention.

_____

Pretty Little CHALLENGE

This week, let God be your teacher and let Him show you the right answers.

WEEK 12

ISOLATION

Have you ever felt all alone, like no one could possibly understand what you were going through? Often times we feel isolated when we go through something. Sometimes things that happen to us or things that we go through make us feel so alone and in despair.

In a room full of people, we can feel like none of them understand. We might fake a smile on the outside, but inside we know that we are desperate for help, desperate for someone to be there, desperate for just one person to reach out.

Family, friends, and coworkers may never be there and understand like you want them to. But God is always right there with you. You are never really alone. He is right there ready to fight every one of your battles for you. He is ready to reassure you that He is right there with you every step of the way.

Isolation is not always a bad thing. Sometimes you need to be alone, just you and God. We need to learn how to depend on God and not man. If every man, woman, and child leave you, you still have God. You still have an anchor that will hold you in the despair of the raging sea. You always have God to hold your hand and you always have Him to get your back. Even if no one else has you, He has you.

Deuteronomy 31:8 "The LORD himself goes before you and will be with you; he will never leave you nor forsake you. Do not be afraid; do not be discouraged."

When you are all alone, take a deep breath, and realize you are not really alone. Let that breath be a reminder that God is right by your side.

Pretty Little CHALLENGE

This week, remember it is God who goes before you and He will be with you step for step.

WEEK 13

BLURRED LINES

The world's culture has forgotten who its Creator is. They have accepted and embraced what God has called sin. They have embraced separation from Him, and their lines between good and evil have been blurred.

Have any lines in your life become blurred? Do you find yourself having a hard time agreeing with everything the Word of God says? We have to take all of the Word of God and not just some of it.

It is time we start taking God's voice seriously. If He convicts us, we need to take the conviction seriously. We need to embrace His voice concerning salvation and conviction. Obedience to conviction protects us. When we obey His voice, we are spared a lot of heartache and frustration.

Do not ignore the still small voice within you. When He corrects us, it is because He loves us. If He did not love us He would not take the time to correct us. Conviction is actually proof of His love.

Just like a good mother and father lay down rules and guidelines, so does our Heavenly Father. His rules are not meant to be broken no matter what anyone says. There are always reasons for His rules. Let us get rid of the excuses of why we don't, or can't obey, and just obey. God has made it plain to us in His Word what is right and what is wrong. Strive to live a life of godliness and not godlessness.

Romans 1:18-20 "The wrath of God is being revealed from heaven against all the godlessness and wickedness of people, who suppress the truth by their wickedness, since what may be known about God is plain to them, because God has made it plain to them. For since the creation of the world God's invisible qualities—his eternal power and divine nature—have been clearly seen, being understood from what has been made, so that people are without excuse."

Let the day of excuses in your life be over. When His voice corrects, hear, listen, and obey.

Pretty Little CHALLENGE

This week, embrace the rules of God and live them out for the entire world to see.

WEEK 14

FORGIVENESS > CONDEMNATION

That last devotional might have been a tough one. This one is going to be easier to digest. The Lord convicts those who love Him; He does not condemn them. You see, people will condemn you when you do wrong, but God will lovingly correct and forgive you.

There might have been times when we have failed and gotten off track. Other people might see us and call us hypocrites. But what they don't know is that we have been wrestling with our issues, trying for a long time to overcome them.

We know our faults and we know the mess we have made of our lives. We don't need any more condemnation from anyone. We are hard enough on ourselves as it is. So what do we do when we fall short? We learn about forgiveness.

God's grace and mercy follow us on a daily basis, making up any lack we may have. When we stumble and fall, Jesus is right there helping us and encouraging us to get back up. Dust yourself off and move toward the mark. Do not allow anyone to condemn you when you are down. Let God forgive you and remind you that you can do better than the sin you are in.

John 8:11 "And Jesus said, "I do not condemn you, either. Go. From now on sin no more."

If your heart condemns you, know that God is greater than even your heart. Go out and forgive and let go of the condemnation you may have for others. You may even have to let go of the condemnation that you have against yourself.

Pretty Little CHALLENGE

This week, remember that the forgiveness of God IS stronger than the condemnation of man.

WEEK 15

FIERCE

When we see someone who is on point we might say they look fierce or they are fierce. We see their fierceness and secretly wish that we could feel just as fierce as they looked.

What does fierce mean anyway? Fierce by definition means extremely intense. If we want to be fierce then we are going to have to be intense for Jesus. Let us not intensify anything else over our intensity of our love for Jesus.

If we are going to be fierce for anyone, let's be fierce for Him. Jesus was so passionate and intense for us unto death that we should be willing to be passionate and intense for Him in life.

Become intense with your prayer and your worship. Praise the Lord and offer up thanksgiving with a fierceness you never have before. Set time aside to intensify your relationship with Him and watch Him intensify the miracles that are produced in your life.

Be on point with the Word of God and you will be fierce! Go to school and work with your head held high because you are a fierce woman of God. This scripture in Song of Solomon is as intense as it gets.

Song of Solomon 8:6 "Place me like a seal over your heart, like a seal on your arm; for love is as strong as death, its jealousy unyielding as the grave. It burns like blazing fire, like a mighty flame."

Place God as a seal upon your heart and a seal upon your arm. Love Jesus more than life itself. Let His love burn within you.

Pretty Little CHALLENGE

This week, step up your intensity for Jesus
in everything you do.

WEEK 16

CELEB STATUS

The "A-listers" who have everyone enticed by their lifestyles are everywhere. We see celebrities where ever we turn. Maybe not in person, but most definitely on television, magazines, online, and on the movie screen.

They travel the world and live larger than life. They have more than enough fame and money to last them the rest of their lives. It is no wonder that people try to imitate them and follow their every move. They live what seems to be the good life and everyone wants to live the good life, right?

But why is it that even the rich and famous seem to struggle with addictions, depression, and suicide? Sometimes they even seem like they have to deal with those issues more than the average person. We must ask ourselves, "Why?"

Why do those who seemingly have it all give up so easily? Why do they struggle so much? They struggle because they are still human no matter how much wealth or fame they get. They still have to deal with negative thoughts and attacks from the enemy. The only real good life is found when we are living for Jesus and are called according to His purpose. When you have the world at your fingertips, you can forget that you need a Savior. You forget the real reason for living. We don't live for celebrities. We don't live for things. We live because God gave us life. We have to be very careful to worship God and not the creation. Serve God, not man. Serve God, not flesh.

Romans 1:25 "They exchanged the truth about God for a lie, and worshiped and served created things rather than the Creator--who is forever praised. Amen."

Don't trade the truth of God for the false promises of the high life. The good life is a godly life, not a worldly life. Serve the Creator rather than the created things. Things will pass through your hands but God is forever.

Pretty Little CHALLENGE

This week, remember who you serve.

WEEK 17

CONFIDENCE

Have you ever seen those women who just ooze confidence? That is how every young woman who believes on Jesus should be. We should have a confidence that is not in ourselves but in our Savior.

Confidence in Him will make us braver than we ever thought we could be. It will make us bolder, stronger, and more assertive. The confidence that comes with Christ is truly amazing and freeing. This confidence is not arrogance but it is a blessed assurance.

We can be confident in our salvation and our purpose. God will give us the confidence to say what needs to be said. We just have to get our flesh out of the way and let God work through us. Always remember in whom your confidence is.

We can be absolutely confident because Jesus made a way for us to be who we were destined to be. Be confident in the fact that you are the daughter of the King of Kings. If your earthly dad is not around or maybe you just do not have a great relationship with him and do not have much confidence in him, you can have great confidence in your Heavenly Father.

Your Heavenly Father is the strongest, greatest, and ablest of all fathers.

Jesus made a way for us to be adopted into the family. Our confidence is not in our own names or in the names of our parents; our confidence is in the name of Jesus.

Ephesians 3:12 "In him and through faith in him we may approach God with freedom and confidence."

Gain confidence by growing in your knowledge of who Jesus is and who you are in Him.

_____

*Pretty Little*CHALLENGE

This week, learn how to ooze confidence in Jesus Christ.

WEEK 18

FAITHFUL

The definition of faithful is loyal, constant, and steadfast. These are all attributes that we expect from family and look for in friends. In relationships we look for someone who will be faithful.

Did you know that God is looking for the same thing? He is looking for someone who will be loyal to Him and His Word. He is looking for someone who will be constant in their faith. It is so crucial that we learn how to become persistent.

Becoming consistent in our faith means we are continually growing, stretching, and working our faith. How do we do that? Our faith grows when we hear the Word of God and allow it to touch our hearts. When we hear the Word, it will minister to us and remind us of things that we need to be reminded.

When we are faithful, we will see just how faithful God is to those who believe. God is looking for someone to show Himself strong on their behalf. He is looking for the faithful and when He finds the faithful, He blesses and protects them. The benefits of being faithful are endless. Faith is how Christians survive. Faith is believing even when you can't see. Faith is trusting God even when you don't have all the answers. If we had the answer to every question we ever had, then there would be no need for faith.

Hebrews 11:6 "Without faith it is impossible to please Him, for he who comes to God must believe that He is, and that He is a rewarder of those who diligently seek Him."

There is a reason He told us to keep the faith. He knew that we would need faith to stay in the race. A relationship of faith is built on trust. The key to your faith is reliant on your trust in Him. God has always been faithful and has given us every reason to trust Him.

Pretty Little CHALLENGE

This week, keep the faith and let God show Himself strong on your behalf!

WEEK 19

TRENDS

Hashtags are everywhere. They are taking over social media. What happens when a lot of people hashtag the same thing? It starts trending; it becomes a trend for the world to see.

What is trending in your life? If your life had a hashtag this week, what would it be? Would it be #bored, #sick, #hurt, #fedup, or one of the many other hashtags out there? Or can you honestly say that your hashtag would be one that is uplifting and encouraging?

Ultimately we are the ones who decide what is trending in our lives. If what trends in our life is always negative we have to take a look at ourselves and quit pointing the finger at everyone else.

It is time to get a godly trend in our lives. Let us start trending the Word of God in our lives. Let praise and worship become a trend. Prayer should become a trend. If we have to remove old trends to make room for the new trends then so be it. We have to take control of the trends in our life. Just because something is trending in someone else's life does not mean it has to trend in ours.

If the trends of your life are already on the right track, keep it up. But if what is trending in your life needs to change then make a change.

Romans 12:2 "Do not conform to the pattern of this world, but be transformed by the renewing of your mind. Then you will be able to test and approve what God's will is."

Renew your mind and get a new trend. The patterns of this world quickly change, but the pattern of God has been tried and is true.

_____

Pretty Little CHALLENGE

This week, get a holy trend that will forever change the way you live.

WEEK 20

COVER GIRL

Easy, breezy, and beautiful, that is what a Cover Girl is. But life is not always easy, breezy, and beautiful. Sometimes life gets down to the nitty-gritty and messy. This life can throw wicked curve balls at even the prettiest of Cover Girls.

How do we handle those things in this life that are totally out of our control? How do we handle the things that are downright ugly? We have learned to trust and we have learned to keep the faith, but what do we do when our easy, breezy, beautiful lives turn into chaos?

When you have done all you can do, you have to stand. And when you have hoped all you can, you have to hope beyond hope. Remind yourself in the hard times that God is still good and does only good.

Job in the Bible had plenty of moments to curse God. His children were killed, his house destroyed, and his own body was attacked with sickness. Instead of cursing God, Job hoped against hope and said, "Though He slay me, yet will I trust Him." We have to get to the point where, when life gives us every reason to give up, that we just don't give up.

We will have to push through hard times and keep our faith alive.

Keep looking to Jesus as your guide through the trouble. He will find you a way out.

John 16:33 "I have told you these things, so that in me you may have peace. In this world you will have trouble. But take heart! I have overcome the world."

Jesus has already overcome anything you face in this life! He overcame it so that you could have the victory through Him. He knew that trouble would come so He becomes our hope in the times of trouble.

Pretty Little CHALLENGE

This week, don't be overcome by this world. Instead be an overcomer through Jesus Christ.

WEEK 21

BAD HAIR DAY

Have you ever had a bad hair day? Some things in life are not major but they still cause plenty of aggravation. Kind of like how a bad hair day can ruin a perfectly good outfit or photo op. No matter how perfect you get everything else, if your hair does not fix like you want it to, it can be very frustrating.

We have to take care of even the little aggravations in our walk with the Lord, because even little tears can cause big rifts. Just like how a small stain on your favorite blouse can cause a big distraction.

Have you noticed that maybe you have not been reading the Bible every day? Have you forgotten to spend one-on-one time with the Lord like you should? Have you let little things get between you and your relationship with God? Has something little caused a rift?

We have to be honest with ourselves and make sure that the little things don't block the big picture. There is a bigger picture that does not focus on the bad hair. This bigger picture is a collection of everyday little things. Make sure that every little part of your life is in God's hands. We have to learn not to let the little things spoil our lives. We also have to let go of the little things that God tells us to let go of, even if we think they are no big deal.

Song of Solomon 2:15 "Catch for us the foxes, the little foxes that ruin the vineyards, our vineyards that are in bloom."

Even the smallest of things can cause great frustrations, just like the small foxes that can ruin large vineyards. Just like a bad hair day can ruin a good mood.

Pretty Little CHALLENGE

This week, look around and see if there has been something little blocking you from something bigger.

WEEK 22

I CAN

As women, many of us, think very harshly about ourselves. We place limits on ourselves that we were never meant to place. By placing limits on ourselves we place limits on what God can do for us. We have to take the limits off!

We have to step outside ourselves and into Christ. We have to get the negative voices out of our heads. We have to replace the "I can'ts" with "I can do all things through Christ who gives me strength."

God will give you the strength that you never thought you could have. He will take you places that you never thought you could go. He will bring dreams to pass that you never thought you could accomplish.

All things are made possible with Him. We can do nothing on our own. When you know that you can't do something reassure yourself by saying, "HE CAN." He can make all things new. He can heal our sick bodies. He can make a way. He can see us through. He is strong when we are weak. We draw our strength from Him. We draw our courage from Him. We are limitless with Him. We must have limitless faith!

He is the only one who can help us and get us to the point where nothing is impossible. He will make our feet sure and steady. He will help us accomplish what we set out to do. He is our "I CAN". He is the great I AM.

Philippians 4:13 "I can do all things through him who gives me strength."

You may not be strong enough, but He is! He will give you strength! If He says you can do it, then you can do it. Replace doubt with faith. Replace fear with trust. God is not setting you up to fail. He is setting you up to succeed through Him. You got this! You can do this!

Pretty Little CHALLENGE

This week, be encouraged to do all things through Christ who gives you strength.

WEEK 23

CAN I GET A WITNESS?

Being a witness is one of our greatest assignments. God wants us to share with others what He has done for us. Our testimony is one of our greatest ministry tools that we have. Testimonies touch hearts because they are personal and show others that God is still working in people's lives today.

It shows people that the God who worked miracles thousands of years ago is still working miracles today. Your friends need to hear your testimony. Your family needs to hear your testimony. They should not only hear it, they should be able to see it. You are literally a walking testimony.

If you are the only one saved in your household God can use you to bring the rest of your family to Christ. The best way for your family to see the love of Christ is through how you love and how you live now that Jesus has saved you.

Be a witness with your words and actions. Testify about how good God has been and show the goodness of the Lord to all those you are believing for their salvation. Your kindness toward others will be a witness. Your faithfulness will be a witness. Your love will be a witness, your diligence will be a witness. Let all that you do be a witness to the lost.

**Psalm 107:2 "Let the redeemed of the Lord
tell their story."**

Time to tell your story! Testify about God's goodness. Let people see and hear how good God has been to you. Have you been redeemed? Then speak out! You are a living witness to the goodness of God. Let's shout from the roof tops that we are the redeemed of the Lord!

 *Pretty Little* CHALLENGE

This week, witness to your family and testify to your friends. Watch how God moves through your testimony and see family and friends saved.

WEEK 24

LIVES OF THE RICH AND FAMOUS

There is an overwhelming infatuation with the rich and famous. There are websites and TV shows dedicated to reporting the news about those who have achieved fame. It is intriguing to see people lose it over meeting someone famous.

There are people whose goal in life is to be famous. They spend countless hours promoting themselves whenever and wherever they can. YouTube and other sources of video media have been a vehicle to make people famous.

The more views a video gets, the more famous the person becomes. What I wonder though is, out of those thousands upon thousands of people who promote themselves, how many of them will promote the name of Jesus just as hard?

We have to make it about the Lord before we make it about ourselves. All glory and fame belongs to God. We were never meant to be set up so high on a pedestal. If your dream is to become famous, ask yourself, why? Is it to give you a platform to be a better witness for Jesus or is it a platform to better promote yourself?

Don't get me wrong, I am not against fame. But you have to be ready for what fame will try to do to you. Fame will eat you up and spit you out without thinking twice about it.

Proverbs 27:21 (Message) "The purity of silver and gold is tested by putting them in the fire; The purity of human hearts is tested by giving them a little fame."

Fame will put your faith and morals to the test. Give God the adoration and glory that belong to Him. Always point your victories back to Christ. Make sure your heart is pure.

Pretty Little CHALLENGE

This week, and every week, promote Jesus over yourself.

WEEK 25

UNASHAMED

Have you ever been so excited about something that you just could not keep it to yourself? When someone is passionate about something there is no stopping them. When we are passionate about something, we are not ashamed to let everyone know about it.

We need to get to the place where we are so passionate about God that we have no shame when it comes to sharing the gospel.

What is the gospel? The gospel is the birth, life, death, and resurrection of Jesus Christ. There should be no shame when you are talking about what Jesus has done, especially what He has done for you.

The culture in which we live tries to take Him out of the school house and the work place but they should never be able to take Him from your heart. I refuse to let anyone shame me into not talking about my Savior.

A young woman from China had a huge impact on my life when she said that the Lord had to protect her because that is the only way she would be able to share the gospel.

Even through threats, she was unashamed of Christ. She knew that the Lord would protect her when she was unashamed of Him.

Romans 1:16 "For I am not ashamed of the gospel, because it is the power of God that brings salvation to everyone who believes."

If we are unashamed then we can make salvation go viral. Jesus was unashamed to die for us, so we can be unashamed to live for Him!

Pretty Little CHALLENGE

This week, walk unashamed of the gospel. Walk the walk and talk the talk with boldness like never before.

WEEK 26

DETOX

When someone says they are detoxing, it means they are cleansing themselves of harmful toxins that have hindered them. It is a time in which a person abstains from certain things to rid the body of unhealthy substances.

It is about to get real, so hold on tight. Some of us may need to detox the relationships that we are involved in. We have been in toxic relationships for too long and they have caused their fair share of harm. Why is it so hard to let go of toxic relationships?

If you see that someone is detrimental to your faith, why would you insist on keeping the relationship intact? If at all possible, cut ties with the toxic people in your life. Toxic people will poison your life. Recognize who is toxic and then steer clear of them.

If you are unable to avoid certain relationships focus on allowing God to show you how to handle the toxins that others produce. God will always make a way to escape the toxins. We can detox in every area of our lives. Detox from harmful secular music. Detox from sin. Detox from being boy crazy. There are so many things we can detox from. God would have us to cleanse ourselves through Christ.

Detoxing may cause discomfort, but that discomfort will leave once the cleanse is complete.

2 Timothy 2:21 (ESV) "Therefore if anyone cleanses himself from what is dishonorable , he will be a vessel for honorable use, set apart as holy, useful to the master of the house, ready for every good work."

It is time to detox yourself from the culture and allow God to clean out the poisons in your life. Spiritually cleanse from the inside out.

Pretty Little CHALLENGE

This week, cleanse yourself of everything that is bad for you by letting Jesus in every part of your life.

WEEK 27

ATTITUDE ADJUSTMENT

It is plain to see when someone needs an attitude adjustment. Their displeasure is usually written all over their faces. You have probably seen someone make a face where you could tell exactly what they are thinking.

One of my favorite sayings is, 'FIX YOUR FACE', which I must admit, I have said to a person or two. But rather than looking at how many other people need attitude adjustments, let's look to see if maybe we ourselves need an adjustment or two, or three, or four.

We may not be able to control everything that happens to us but we can control how we respond to everything. Our attitude concerning every situation that comes our way is entirely up to us.

We can be negative or we can be positive. We can be the pessimist, opportunist, or the optimist. We have the chance to choose our attitude. Instead of talking back to mom and dad, we can show respect. Instead of smart mouthing our least favorite teacher, we can bite our tongue.

Our face reads our heart and then reflects it, so we need to fix our face.

Proverbs 27:19 "As water reflects the face, so one's life reflects the heart."

Getting your heart right will fix your face for you. Your attitude reflects your heart. You cannot adjust everyone else's attitude, but you can adjust your own. You are in charge of how you respond to things. Your attitude is entirely up to you. Refuse to let your circumstance dictate your attitude. Instead let faith determine how you act.

Pretty Little CHALLENGE

This week, fix your heart so that you can fix your attitude.
Embrace God's attitude adjustment for your life.

WEEK 28

CRAZY IN LOVE

Love will make you do incredible and sometimes crazy things. Love has caused men to start wars and end them. Women have shown incredible feats of strength protecting those they love. Love will drive us, love will keep us, and love will sustain us.

Most of us would do just about anything for those that we love. We would sacrifice for them and give all we have for them. God showed His crazy love for us by sending Jesus to die for us. He set an example of love for us. What have we done to show our crazy love for Him?

If we do crazy things for those that we love here on earth, how much more should we do for God? If we love Him, we will keep His commandments. We will sacrifice for Him and give all we have to Him.

When we are crazy in love with Jesus, our love is undeniable. You will be able to see our love for Him at every turn we make.

His love is what drives us toward our purpose. His love is what keeps us on track. His love is what sustains us through the bad. His love is our everything. Some may call us crazy, but we are not crazy, we are crazy in love.

Luke 10:27 "Love the Lord your God with all your heart and with all your soul and with all your strength and with all your mind."

That is a lot of love! We are to love Him from the depths of our souls and the deepest part of our hearts. We have to love Him more than we love anyone and anything else. Our love for Him should be the realest thing in our lives.

Pretty Little CHALLENGE

This week, fall in love with Jesus all over again. Have a crazier love for Him than you ever have before.

WEEK 29

THE IMPOSSIBLE

If you have ever faced an impossible situation then you know the helplessness that comes with the impossible. The impossible situations in our lives test and try our faith. Impossibilities can wreak havoc on the mind and the soul.

But when we study the Bible, we see numerous miracles where Jesus makes the impossible possible. We see it when He heals the lame man. We see it when He raises Lazarus from the dead. We see it when He makes the barren produce.

Impossibilities are just opportunities for Jesus to work a miracle in your life. Will you let your faith answer the impossible? Jesus can make a way where there is no way. He can bring peace in the midst of the storm. He can deliver us out of even the most hopeless and desperate of situations.

If you ever find yourself in an impossible situation, remember who your God is. God is able! He can heal you. He can restore your family. He can deliver the addicted. He can set free the oppressed. When no one can, HE CAN!

Not only is God able, but He is also willing to help you through the impossible. He can make a way where there is no way. He can even open doors that man tried to close in your life.

Mark 10:27 "Jesus looked at them and said, 'With man this is impossible, but with God; all things are possible with God."

What an awesome scripture. This is just one of those scriptures that we should memorize and hold in our hearts. With man there will always be impossibilities, but with God all things are possible.

Pretty Little CHALLENGE

This week, when you pray, believe and receive the endless possibilities that you have in Jesus. Remember man is not your way maker, Jesus is! Give Him the impossible!

WEEK 30

BLESSED

Have you ever wondered why some people seem to be more blessed than others? Blessing is tied to obedience. Obedience brings blessing. To obey is better than sacrifice.

It is when we take heed to the statutes that the Lord has given that we are truly blessed. God's commands come with great rewards. We need to stop looking at things we should not do as a loss and start to look at all of the gains when we obey. We gain so much when we listen and obey.

We can only be obedient to what we know. That is why it is so important that you dig deep into the Word of God to find His promises. God keeps every one of His promises. We have to obey the command to receive the promise that is connected.

The Word was given to be a blessing for all those who believe on what it says. In the Bible there are so many blessings that one devotional could not contain them all.

God blesses the faithful. He blesses the obedient. He blesses those who give. He blesses those who serve. He is a rewarder to those who diligently seek Him. He has more than enough to bless every believer with an overflow of blessing. He wants us blessed coming in and blessed going out.

Revelation 1:3 "Blessed is the one who reads aloud the words of this prophecy, and blessed are those who hear it and take to heart what is written in it, because the time is near."

The time is nearer now than it has ever been. We must take to heart every verse God gives us. We have to take it to heart and live it out to be blessed.

Pretty Little CHALLENGE

This week, find out what God says and then take it to heart. When you do this, you will be blessed beyond measure.

WEEK 31

ANXIETY

Anxiety - the unpleasant state of inner turmoil. Anxiety can cause hearts to race and can even cause panic attacks. It can be brought about by an overwhelming sense of fear or an intense amount of stress within the mind.

I have seen someone in a normal setting with no real triggers for anxiety and, all of a sudden, a panic attack sets in. Something within their minds and hearts took them to a place of anxiety. How do we take control over the anxiety?

God does not want us to be anxious for anything. He wants us to come to Him in prayer with everything so that we will not be anxious in our minds and hearts. We can take control of anxiety by giving up control of anxiety.

What I mean by that is that we need to give everything to God that would make us anxious. God knew that we would have cares in this life. He knew there would be stress that we would have to overcome. Even the routines of life can become stressful and make us anxious if we don't give God control. Remember God is in control when you give Him control. If we keep taking matters into our own hands, we will become anxious. We can't do this on our own; we need Him.

1 Peter 5:7 "Cast all your anxiety on him because he cares for you."

God cares enough about you to deliver you from the anxiety within you. Give God your anxious mind and your anxious heart. Let God be your stress reliever. When anything would try to trigger anxiety on the inside of you, take a deep breath and give God control.

Pretty Little CHALLENGE

This week, cast all your anxiety on Him and feel the weight lifted off your shoulders.

WEEK 32

INSOMNIA

One of the worst feelings that I have ever experienced is when I laid my head down at night and I could not sleep. My mind would race with all the things that had to be done the next day. Fear would try to eat away at the last few hours that I had to fall asleep.

It would literally take me hours to try to fall asleep. When the alarm sounded in the morning I was exhausted because when I did eventually fall asleep I would still toss and turn. Have you ever experienced anything similar?

If you have, there is hope! The possibility of a good night's sleep is right around the corner. God wants to be our rest. He will be the cool shade on a hot summer's day. He will gather us under His wing and comfort and protect us.

He wants all who are weary and heavy hearted to come to Him so that He can give them rest. The rest He gives is peaceful. It will cause you to wake up to righteousness. When your alarm clock sounds, you can get up feeling well rested and full of life. There will be less and less days of waking up on the wrong side of the bed.

There are enough things in this world that would try to steal your rest. Get it all back. Let your heart be glad and let your body rest secure in Christ. You can and will find rest in God alone.

Proverbs 3:24 "When you lie down, you will not be afraid; when you lie down, your sleep will be sweet."

Wouldn't it be nice to lie down and your sleep be sweet? Have you been ready for a long time to get to that place? Tonight is the night for your sleep to be sweet!

Pretty Little CHALLENGE

This week, rest in the Lord and your sleep will be sweet.

WEEK 33

GOSSIPERS

There is probably no one in the world who really enjoys being talked badly about. When others talk behind our backs, it makes us feel vulnerable and can hurt to the depths of our hearts. We all have, at one point, probably been gossiped about and also have been a gossiper.

Gossip has been the bane of every girl's existence since time began. It ruins and spoils friendships that were built for years in a split second. In a blink of an eye, gossip can change even the strongest of relationships.

Gossip is not always taken as seriously as it should be. Sometimes we think it is harmless because we think the other person will never find out. But we all know that they eventually find out.

When gossip starts, we have to be quick to either change the subject or walk away. Gossip will eat away at your life if you let it. It will ruin lives if we let it. Gossip just adds fuel to the fire. When gossip stops, so does the fighting.

Avoid gossip at every turn. Catch yourself before you open up your mouth to gossip. Steer clear of gossipers.

Proverbs 20:19 "A gossip betrays a confidence; so avoid a man who talks too much."

Girls like to talk, so be careful and know when it is time to stop talking. Do not betray a friend by talking about them. Do not even gossip about enemies. Let the Lord take care of the enemies in your life. Know when to walk away from the gossip. And if anyone is gossiping about you, learn to have a tender heart toward God and a thick skin toward people who gossip about you.

Pretty Little CHALLENGE

This week, stand your ground against gossip.

WEEK 34

REVENGE

Have you ever had someone who did you wrong and you want so badly to get revenge on them? There are plenty of opportunities to seek revenge on those who have done you wrong, but revenge is not the answer.

Revenge might be gratifying for a moment but it will make you pay too. We think that revenge will only hurt the other person, but it will most definitely hurt us as well. Revenge has the potential to destroy the people we love. Is revenge really worth it?

We are not to avenge ourselves. The Lord says that vengeance is His. What does that mean? God will take care of the people who do you wrong. We all have to answer for what we do. Allow the Lord to make the wrong right.

Two wrongs do not make a right. Just because someone does you wrong does not mean you have to do them wrong. You are better than that. Rise above the need for revenge. If you say you will get them back for their wrong, you are just as wrong as they are. Let go of the grudges. Get rid of the hate. Let the Lord be your vengeance.

Leviticus 19:18 "Do not seek revenge or bear a grudge against anyone among your people, but love your neighbor as yourself."

We have to learn to understand that the grudges we hold against others really only hurt us in the end. The key to letting go of revenge is quick forgiveness. It is when we linger on things that bitterness and revenge are birthed. Vengeance is the Lord's!

Pretty Little CHALLENGE

This week, let God handle those who have done evil against you. Work on forgiving so that you don't take matters into your own hands by seeking revenge.

WEEK 35

NO MORE CHAINS

Chains of this life will weigh us down. Chains can represent a multitude of things in this life. Some chains are physical like addictions and sickness. Other chains can be much harder to see because they are invisible, internal chains that bind us on the inside.

Breaking free from the chains is impossible on our own. We will need help from God to be delivered from everything that binds us. The good news is that God is in the business of breaking chains.

God gives us freedom from the chains when we cry out to Him and seek His help. We all too often try to free ourselves from the chains, as if we could pick the lock to our own struggles. The reason we get bound is because we can't free ourselves.

Jesus is the key to every chain that binds you. Jesus is the key to your breakthrough. Jesus is the key to your healing. Jesus is your key to happiness. Jesus is your key to freedom. For every chain, Jesus is the answer. No one really wants to be bound. Get tied up in Jesus so you don't get tied up in anything else.

Psalm 107:14 "He brought them out of darkness and the deepest gloom and broke away their chains."

God will break away the chains when you call out to Him. No matter how far you think you have drifted off, He can free you when you cry out. When anything binds you, immediately take authority over it by calling Him to help you.

Pretty Little CHALLENGE

This week, cry out to Jesus so He can
break away your chains.

WEEK 36

INVISIBLE

Have you ever felt invisible to people? When you walk into the room, do you still feel like no one really sees you? Maybe you have felt like your voice has not been heard lately. Or maybe people are not taking you as seriously as you would like them to.

Sometimes we can feel like our opinion does not even matter to anyone. What you think might not matter to anyone else, but it does matter to God. What you think about yourself and what you think about God does matter.

You are not invisible to God. He sees you and can hear you when you pray. You matter to Him more than you could ever know. The issues of your life are not invisible to Him either. He sees and knows what you are going through. He knows you by name. He has numbered the very hairs upon your head. He knows your personal storm and is your peace in the midst of it.

He knows you better than you know yourself. He knows your heart and your intentions. He sees you for who you really are. When you walk into His presence, He will not ignore you. He will treat you like the daughter that you are to Him. God sees every one of those tears that you have cried. He sees every broken piece of your heart. He knows what happened to you. He knew you before you were even born. He sees you and keeps track of you.

Psalm 56:8 (NLT) "You keep track of my sorrows. You have collected all my tears in your bottle."

He sees your tears, He sees your triumphs, He sees your life, HE SEES YOU! If you are somewhere and you feel insignificant and unimportant, remember you are important and significant to God.

Pretty Little CHALLENGE

This week, remind yourself that you are not invisible, God sees you.

WEEK 37

PERFECTION

No one is perfect, it is true. But Jesus was and is absolutely perfect. He made a way for us to have perfection in Him and in Him alone. We are made perfect in the blood of Jesus Christ.

Our perfection is not in outward appearance but in our striving to be like Christ. If there is anything in this life that concerns us, He wants to perfect it. If it is our past that concerns us, He perfects it with His blood. If it is a sickness that concerns us, He perfects it by His stripes. If it is family that concerns us, He perfects it with giving us hope for their salvation.

In an imperfect world He is our perfection. There is no one like Him. There is nothing that can compare to Him. He is the name that is above all names. He is perfect and will perfect that which concerns us.

If we know that our concerns will be perfected in Him then we need to learn to give Him our concerns. From silly, small concerns to crazy, big concerns, He can perfect them. Those concerns that keep you up at night can be perfected. Those concerns that you feel in the pit of your stomach can be perfected.

Psalm 138:8 "The Lord will perfect that which concerneth me..."

In the hands of God your concerns can be made perfect through Him. Always remember we are not perfect on our own. We need Jesus to help us get it right.

Pretty Little CHALLENGE

This week, let the Lord perfect your concerns regarding E-V-E-R-Y-T-H-I-N-G!

WEEK 38

WORRY

When we are uneasy and troubled about something that means we are worried. When we worry it means that we are lacking faith. When we worry it means we have doubts about God's ability to see us through.

We might never say that we doubt God but that is exactly what worry is. Doubt steals faith. Worry steals time. We gain nothing by worrying. We gain everything by faith. Worry will not add any hours to your life.

Research has shown that most things that people worry about will never happen in the first place. So we spend all that time worrying about something that will never happen. Worry is absolutely a waste of your time. We do not have time to waste.

Replace worry with faith. Replace doubt with hope. Go to God about what worries you. Go to God when you think about bad things that might happen to you. Every day has its own set of complications. Take one day at a time with God by your side. Let the *'what am I going to do's?'* turn into the *'I know God has got me.'*

Matthew 6:34 (ISV) "So never worry about tomorrow, because tomorrow will worry about itself. Each day has enough trouble of its own."

God holds your future so there is no need to worry about all the tomorrows. Plan ahead but don't worry. Don't worry, be happy.

Pretty Little CHALLENGE

This week, focus on taking one day at a time and appreciating every second of it instead of worrying about every part of it.

WEEK 39

RED CARPET

It is time to roll out the red carpet. Preparation has been made to get all glammed up. Hair is done, make-up is done. The dress fits perfectly, the jewelry is divine. The flashes of light from the cameras are everywhere. We step out on the red carpet and in our first interview they ask, "*Who are you wearing?*"

Quick, think on your feet, *who are you wearing*? Do you have an answer? We are to put on Christ and represent Him every minute of every day. He gives us a robe of righteousness to wear and full armor to protect. The armor He gives us protects us from the worst of attacks.

The armor that He gives is found in His Word (Ephesians 6). What we should wear every single day is faith, peace, truth, righteousness, salvation, and the Spirit. What we wear on our spirit is the most important dress we will ever wear.

This wardrobe is made by the Designer, Alpha and Omega.

He is the beginning and the end. He gives us these fashions to keep the faith! People will notice the light that shines within you. When someone asks us who we are wearing, we had better have an answer. When they ask why we hope, we need to have an answer. When they ask why we are not afraid, we need to have an answer.

1 Peter 3:15 "But in your hearts revere Christ as Lord. Always be prepared to give an answer to everyone who asks you to give a reason for the hope that you have. But do this with gentleness and respect."

We have to be ready to give an answer when they notice the hope that is on the inside of us. We should have a hope that stands out for other people to see. When we put on Christ, we put on hope. He is our righteousness and He is our hope! Next time they ask you a question, be ready with an answer from the Word of God.

Pretty Little CHALLENGE

This week, put on the full armor of God and be ready to give an answer for your hope!

WEEK 40

WHO CARES?

Does it sometimes feel like no one cares what you are going through? The most important thing to understand is that God cares whether anyone else on earth cares or not. He cares!

He cares so much that He gave His one and only begotten Son to die on a cross so that you could have everlasting life. He cares so much that He will heal you when you are sick, deliver you when you are addicted, and strengthen you when you are weak. He is your help in the time of trouble. He cares so much for you that He wrote out a plan for your life. He cares so much for you that He will restore every part of you.

We have to trust Him to be able to feel that care He has for us. God cares about every trial you face and every obstacle that stands in your way. He cares that you are hurting. He cares that you are slipping away from Him. He cares that your heart is broken.

There is not one part of your life that He does not care about. He cares about even the smallest of details when it comes to you. You may not be cared for like you want to be cared for by people, but God cares more than anyone ever could anyway. The next time someone says, "Who cares?", in your heart, know that God cares!

When you feel like no one really cares remember that is a lie, because God absolutely cares.

Nahum 1:7 "The Lord is good, a refuge in the times of trouble. He cares for those who trust Him…"

To feel cared for, you must trust God. He really does care about your life and what you are going through. Turn to Him and trust Him for He cares for you like no one else can.

Pretty Little CHALLENGE

This week, remember who really cares about you. You have a Father who cares a tremendous amount for you!

WEEK 41

KARMA

What goes around comes around. Did you know that the Bible talks about karma? It may not call it by the same name, but it is the same concept. It is the law of sowing and reaping.

When we sow something, that means we are spiritually planting something. When you sow kindness, you reap kindness. When you sow friendliness, you reap friendliness. When you sow righteousness, you reap unfailing love. When you sow the wind, you reap the whirlwind. When you sow sin, you reap death. Well, that escalated pretty quickly, didn't it? But it is true. We have to watch what we are planting into our lives because we will harvest what we plant.

What we put in is what we will get out. God can work things out for your favor when you sow obedience. He makes all things work together for the good to those who love Him and are called according to His purpose. When we are called according to His purpose, we will plant seeds of faith in our lives. When you plant those seeds of faith, you will reap a harvest of miracles!

**Galatians 6:7 (ESV) "Do not be deceived: God is not mocked, for whatever one sows,
that will he also reap..."**

Everyone will have to give an account of what they sowed in this life. That is why it is so good that Jesus sowed on our behalf. We get to benefit from what He has planted!

Pretty Little CHALLENGE

This week, watch what you are sowing in your own life and the lives of others.

WEEK 42

SHAKE IT OFF

Rejection is probably one of the worst feelings that someone can go through. When we are rejected, it can hurt to the very core of who we are. In this life the majority of us will be rejected at one time or another.

I remember playing sports in high school and getting cut from the volleyball team because I was not tall enough. I was rejected because of something that I could not help. It made me sad and even a little angry. Rejection hurts.

We can get help from the Lord when we get rejected. Did you know that when Jesus was on earth, He went to His own people and they rejected Him? Jesus knows what it is like firsthand to be rejected.

Unfortunately, people are still rejecting Him to this very day. So what does He tell us to do when we are rejected? He tells us to shake it off. Not everyone is going to like us and that is okay. Not everyone will approve of us, but as long as we have God's approval, that is all we need. When you come to Him, He will not reject you. He will embrace you with open arms.

There will be times when you try to share the love of Jesus and people will reject you. But realize they are not really rejecting you, they are rejecting Christ.

Matthew 10:14 "If anyone will not welcome you or listen to your words, leave that home or town and shake the dust off your feet."

When they don't like you, shake it off. When they will not listen, shake it off. When they reject you, shake it off. Just shake off the heaviness of rejection and rejoice in the Lord.

Pretty Little CHALLENGE

This week, do not let rejection consume you. Shake it off!

WEEK 43

FLAWLESS

There is not much here on earth that is really truly flawless because of the fall of man. Flawless means without blemish and without imperfections. It would be nice to live in a flawless world, but we will have to wait until we get into Heaven for that one.

Jesus is the only one who is truly flawless. He is without spot and blemish. He washes away our blemishes in His perfection. He gives us His flawlessness to cover ourselves with and washes us white as snow. No matter how terrible our past, we are seen as righteous in God's sight because of Jesus.

Not only do we have our flawless Savior, but we have also been given God's flawless Word. Everything that is found in His Word is true. It has been tested. It has been tried. It has been found to be the truth in every century.

God has protected His Word so that we may be able to cling to it and survive the flaws of this world. His Word will correct any flaws that are found in your heart. If there is anything to reproof, He will reprove it. He will protect us from the flaws of others. He is our refuge and our strong tower.

Proverbs 30:5 "Every word of God is flawless; he is a shield to those who take refuge in Him."

Get rid of flawed thinking and get faith thinking. Hold on to those promises! Those promises He gave you are true. Everything He says is flawless. You can count on His Word. By His Word the world was framed.

Pretty Little CHALLENGE

This week, rely on His flawlessness.
Hold on to His flawless Word!

WEEK 44

CODE BLUE

If you have ever watched a show that is based on what happens in hospitals, you may have heard the phrase, *'code blue.'* Code blue is what the nurse or doctor will say when the patient's heart has stopped. They are flatlining. They are at the brink of death.

We are often faced with spiritual 'code blues'. What do we do when our hearts condemn us? What do we do when we feel like we are slipping away? When we are at a code blue, we have a heart issue.

That is why it is so important to ask God to create in us a clean heart. Our heart is what keeps us going through the worst of situations. The enemy will constantly try to attack your heart through outward assaults.

Boys will try to steal your heart. People might hurt your heart. Life may make your heart feel heavy. So we must learn how to guard our hearts no matter what. Our hearts belong to God. The chains of this life belong at the foot of the cross and not around your heart.

We have to hide the Word of God in our hearts so that we don't sin against Him. We have to guard our hearts so that the issues of life don't overtake us and make us flat line. You see, you can sit in church and your heart really not be there. We have to remember to be all in with our hearts.

Proverbs 4:23 (NLT) "Guard your heart above all else, for it determines the course of your life."

Guard who and what you allow into your heart. Whatever consumes your thoughts will consume your heart. Let God consume your mind so He can help you protect your heart. Put the Word in your heart. Lean not to your own understanding and give God control of your heart. God is the strength of your heart! Allow God to operate on your heart. He is the only one who can revive you.

Pretty Little CHALLENGE

This week, give God ALL of your heart,
every last pretty little piece of it.

WEEK 45

STICKS & STONES

Sticks and stones break bones and words hurt worse than sticks and stones. Words pierce the hearts of those who hear them one way or another. Words can bring life and words can bring death.

We have to be very careful what we allow ourselves to say. We have to really think before we speak. The Bible says that out of the abundance of the heart a man speaks.

Do you allow negativity to spew out of your mouth or do you keep your words positive? It really is a good rule to not say anything at all if you do not have something nice to say.

We must learn to filter our words. We can have opinions, but that does not mean we have to say every last single one of them. We should not be hasty when it comes to our words. We should speak with wisdom and avoid foolish talking.

Our words have so much power in our lives. Blessing and cursing should not proceed out of the same mouth.

Say what you mean and mean what you say. The right word at the right time can change someone's life forever. Your words have more power than you know.

Ephesians 4:29 (ESV) "Let no corrupting talk come out of your mouths, but only such as is good for building up, as fits the occasion, that it may give grace to those who hear."

Don't be careless with your words. Remember what you say has the power to bring hurt or healing. The tongue is unruly so we must learn how to master it. What you say matters.

Pretty Little CHALLENGE

This week, filter your words. Let your words bring life to everyone who hears them.

WEEK 46

DARE TO DREAM

If God has placed a dream inside of you then hold on to that dream. Keep that dream alive and trust that it will come to pass. He gave you that dream for a reason. If He gave it to you then He will make a way for it to come true.

Your dream should turn into a passion then that passion should turn into a mission. Work toward making your godly dream a reality. Work hard toward your goals and you will achieve them.

Dreams and visions take place in your mind and heart, but God will let you hold them in your hand. He is able to bring to pass every last one of your dreams. We have to trust Him with our dreams and trust that He knows the right timing for our dreams to manifest.

Great things are in store for you. God has big plans for each and every one of us. Eye has not seen and ear has not heard the great things He has for us. Pursue your dream by pursuing God first. Make God and His Kingdom the priority and He will take care of your dream.

Has God given you vision for your future? Is He directing your dream? You are destined for such great things. Allow God to be in control of what you pursue in your life. Make sure that your dreams align with His dreams.

Acts 2:17 "In the last days, God says, I will pour out my Spirit on all people. Your sons and daughters will prophesy, your young men will see visions, your old men will dream dreams."

Hold on to your dream. It is not too late for your dream to come true. Remind yourself that if God gave you a dream, He will see it to pass.

Pretty Little CHALLENGE

This week, dare to dream and trust God to bring to pass the dreams He has placed in you.

WEEK 47

SIMPLE ACT OF KINDNESS

You never know what your one simple act of kindness could do for someone. There have been reports of people who had been suicidal that decided not to commit suicide because of one person's simple act of kindness. A simple smile could impact someone's life forever.

Kindness is the key that restores hope for humanity. There are so many ways that we can show kindness to others. Simple gestures like a smile, to helping the elderly carry their groceries, are ways to show kindness. The acts of kindness that we can show are endless.

Next time you grimace at someone, think twice. You never know what someone else is going through. Maybe they just need a little bit of kindness. Be kind to others like God has been kind to you.

Chances are, you won't regret being kind, but you will probably regret being rude. Being rude does not get you very far with people. Being kind can take you places.

Ephesians 4:32 "Be kind and compassionate to one another, forgiving each other, just as Christ forgave you."

A simple act of kindness can turn your day around. When we are kind to others it makes us feel better about ourselves too. The benefit of kindness is so much better than the persona of rudeness. You attract more bees with honey than you do with vinegar. Be sweet by being kind.

---

*Pretty Little*CHALLENGE

This week, challenge yourself to be kind to everyone in all ways.

WEEK 48

BREAKTHROUGH

You may be at a place in your life where you need a breakthrough. Maybe you need God to breakthrough barriers in your life. Maybe you need to breakthrough to your miracle. Hold on just a little while longer. Your breakthrough is on its way.

We have to position ourselves to receive breakthrough by getting into God's Word. We will see in His Word that when we pray, praise, worship, and fast, our breakthrough is coming. It is when we get into His presence that we are assured of our breakthrough.

Our breakthrough is never far off when we are in His presence. He Himself is our breakthrough. He is everything we need and has everything we need to get to the other side.

The rivers they told us we would never cross and the mountains they told us we would never climb are now a part of our breakthrough. We are going to make it to the other side. Do not give up now. Push just a little further. Dig just a little deeper. Your breakthrough is right around the corner.

Keep moving forward. Like Dory, from Finding Nemo, would sing, *"JUST KEEP SWIMMING."*

Eventually you will make it to where you are going if you just keep moving.

Galatians 6:9 "Let us not become weary in doing good, for at the proper time we will reap a harvest if we do not give up."

Don't get tired on Him now. He has never failed you. He has never forsaken you. The harvest is coming! Hold on tight, the breakthrough is about to arrive in your life.

Pretty Little CHALLENGE

This week, get into His presence and receive a blessed assurance of your breakthrough. It is coming!

WEEK 49

A MILLION MILES AWAY

Have you ever felt like God was a million miles away? This life and culture has a way of trying to distance you from God. The flesh is always at war with the spirit. Sin separates us from God. Sometimes when we need God the most, He feels so far away.

Why? The reason this happens is because we focus more on the problem than we focus on God. In the Bible it was when people cried out to God that He was able to save them. They cried out and He delivered them. They cried out and He made a way for them. They cried out and He protected them.

God is only as far away from you as a cry out. He is with you in the good and He is with you in the bad. We have to quit ignoring His presence. He is not far removed from us and He is not far removed from our situations. He is close to those who need Him. He is close to the brokenhearted. He is close to you!

James 4:8 "Come near to God and He will come near to you."

If you listen closely and get into His Word, you will hear a still small voice within your heart reassuring you and comforting you. Even when we push God away, He is still listening for us to cry out, waiting for us to draw near to Him. He is never a million miles away from us. The question we must ask ourselves is if we are a million miles away from Him. There is a difference.

Pretty Little CHALLENGE

This week, draw near to God and He will draw near to you. He will get as close to you as you let Him.

WEEK 50

PERSPECTIVE

How do you view this life? How do you view yourself? How do you view God? These are all questions that deal with your perspective, your point of view. Quietly answer them to yourself right now.

Does your view of this life match what God said this life should be? Do you see yourself as the Lord sees you? Do you really see God for who He is?

We have to get a new perspective on things. We have to get a God perspective. God has the vantage point of knowing the beginning from the end. He is Alpha and He is Omega. He is the Author and the Finisher. It would benefit you to see things from His point of view.

Everything does not make sense to us because we do not have all the facts, but God does. He can make sense of our lives. He can make sense of who we are, He is the one who created us, after all. He really does have every answer that you need. The Bible says that some things are not for us to know right now.

That is where our perspective of faith comes in. His ways are higher than our ways; His thoughts are higher than ours. We must not lean on our own understanding. We have to be able to trust God's perspective.

Psalm 61:2 "From the ends of the earth I call to you, I call as my heart grows faint; lead me to the rock that is higher than I."

Get a better vantage point. Go to the Rock! He is the Rock that we can stand on. He is the Rock with the better perspective. He can make us see things that are unseen. When we stand on His Word and see how He sees, we have a better outlook. Bottom line in everything is do you trust God? Do you trust He knows what He is doing? No matter what it looks like, declare: I TRUST GOD.

*Pretty Little*CHALLENGE

This week, look to God to gain perspective. See God as stronger, greater, and bigger than your problem. He is!

WEEK 51

VINE

Don't set off on your own. You are not in this life alone and you don't have to go it alone. Follow after Jesus and you will not be led astray. He will order your steps and direct your path.

God understands exactly where you are, and He knows exactly where you need to be. Sometimes it is wise to disconnect with people, but it is never wise to disconnect with God. No one on this earth can cut your tether to Christ; only you have the power to do that.

Every day you wake up, you have a decision to make. You decide who you will be, where you will go, and what you will do. Do you consider Christ when making those decisions?

So what does all this have to do with a vine? He is the vine and we are the branches. We were never meant to survive alone. We were always meant to stay with Him. When we were separated from Him, He ripped the veil so that we could be with Him again. Without Him we cannot do what we are supposed to do. Without Him we are not producing fruit like He wants us to.

The vine is what keeps us alive. The vine is what gives us nutrients to produce. The vine is our connection and the reason for breathing.

John 15:4 "Remain in me, as I also remain in you. No branch can bear fruit by itself; it must remain in the vine. Neither can you bear fruit unless you remain in me."

Stay on the vine! We can't make it without the vine. Remain in Christ and He will remain in you. You have the power to stay and the choice to leave. Choose to stay. We need Him more than ever. We need Him to accomplish His purpose in us and through us. He is all that we need. We should not branch out on our own without Him. He is the vine, we are the branches.

This week, attach yourself to the vine and understand that you need Him if you want to thrive.

WEEK 52

THE AFTER PARTY

This is what we have looked forward to. This is what we have all been waiting for. This is the reason why we hope. This is the after party.

When everything is all said and done... When this life is over... What is next? Victory is next. As believers we hold on to the hope of a better day, a better tomorrow. We have a hope for a future with Jesus Christ in heaven.

With the state of the world like it is today, life can be daunting. But that is why we cling to hope. We cling to the hope that one day everything will be better than it is now. One day there will be peace. One day there will be no famine and no war. There will be a day where there is no room for fear because love has taken its spot.

The Bible warned us about the last days. God told us to hold on and to be patient. We must be joyful in hope, patient in affliction, and faithful in prayer. We must let patience have her perfect work in us. We will face trials of many kinds, but we shall overcome them all in Jesus name!

There is coming a time for a new heaven and a new earth, where everything is made right. Justice will be served and faithfulness will be rewarded. When you get saved through Jesus Christ, your name is written down in the Lamb's

Book of Life and you will partake in the goodness of heaven. We will get to see the streets of gold and the gates of pearl. But the best part is that we will be able to see Him face to face.

Revelation 21:4 "He will wipe every tear from their eyes. There will be no more death or mourning or crying or pain, for the old order of things has passed away."

I don't want to miss that after party for anything! I have to let nothing separate me from the love of God. If I want an invite, I need to stay with Jesus. He is my ticket in. He is our hope. He is our source. There will be a day!

This week, hold on to the promise of Heaven. Hold on to the hope of a final victory where you get to see Jesus face to face.

Pretty Little

BONUS
DEVOTIONALS

FALLING APART

Has your life ever seemed like it was falling apart? Maybe like the walls of life were caving in on you, or you felt like you were crumbling within yourself?

Truth is, most of us have been there. Boyfriends will break up with you, friends will leave you (or stab you in the back), and family will fail you. Just because these things happen does not mean that your entire world has to fall apart.

You have so much more going for you than any one person could give you. You have Jesus! There are so many songs that say that He is all you need. But do you believe that?

You have to believe that Jesus is really all you need to make it through. When your world seems to be falling apart, let God hold you together.

**Psalm 91:7 "A thousand may fall at your side,
ten thousand at your right hand,
but it will not come near you."**

———————————————

Pretty Little CHALLENGE ~ You won't fall apart

when Jesus is the one holding you together!

FORGIVE YOURSELF

So you have made some mistakes. Haven't we all? We are not the mistakes that we have made. Those mistakes are what help us to learn. Learn from your past; do not dwell on it. He can turn your past into the strength of your testimony.

Let it go. Forgive yourself for what you have done. If God almighty can forgive you, then you can forgive yourself. Grow from where you used to be. Stand up tall with your head held high and forgive yourself.

We can't grow without change. Change your old ways. Change how you talk. Change how you walk. You are a new creature in Christ; old things have passed away, and all things have become new. You are the NEW YOU!

Philippians 3:13-14 "I do not consider myself yet to have taken hold of it. But one thing I do: Forgetting what is behind and straining toward what is ahead, I press on toward the goal to win the prize for which God has called me heavenward in Christ Jesus."

Pretty Little CHALLENGE ~ Forgive yourself, keep moving toward the goal. He has called you heavenward in

Christ Jesus!

HUNGER GAMES

Whatever you feed will grow. If you spend the most time feeding your flesh then your flesh will be stronger than your spirit. But if you spend the most time feeding your spirit then the spirit will be stronger.

Physical strength is good for a season, but it is spiritual strength that will get you to the end. What are you most hungry for? The things of this world or the things of God?

Like a deer pants for water, so our souls should pant after God. Your hunger will drive you one way or another. Your hunger will yell at you from the inside. Our appetites will not be satisfied until they get what they crave.

What do you crave? Do you crave to be like Christ? Do you crave the Word of God? Do you crave righteousness? If you do, then you will be driven by it.

Matthew 5:6 "Blessed are those who hunger and thirst for righteousness, for they will be filled."

Pretty Little CHALLENGE ~ Be satisfied when you learn to hunger after the right things.

HIS PLAN

Have you mapped out a plan for your life? Have you made a mental list of things that you want to accomplish by certain ages?

If you have, then you are not alone. That is just what young women do. It is good to set up goals for yourself. But sometimes plans change. What do you do when things don't work out like you planned them?

We have to stick to God's plan. His plan for us is better than any of our plans could ever be. He can navigate through every situation in our lives and always get us back to His plan.

Let God's plan overrule your plan!

Jeremiah 29:11 "For I know the plans I have for you," declares the LORD, "plans to prosper you and not to harm you, plans to give you hope and a future."

_____

Pretty Little CHALLENGE ~ His plan never fails!

Stick to the plan that He wrote and you will accomplish

things that are greater than you ever imagined.

ANGER MANAGEMENT

Anger is the sneaky little villain that tries to creep up on us all. Think the Hulk. One minute he is okay and then, all of a sudden, something sets him off. Something on the outside caused the rage to build up on the inside.

Have you ever had that happen? Most of us have. Anger has the ability to eat away at our lives. It can cause bitterness and strife. It can cause bursts of rage and make us say things we would normally never have said.

Anger is a natural emotion that we all have to deal with and put in its place. The Bible says to be angry and sin not. How do we do that? We do that by not letting the anger take over. We do that by allowing God to be in charge even when we are angry. Learn what is worth the fight and what isn't worth the fight.

Ephesians 4:26 (NLT) "Don't sin by letting anger control you. Don't let the sun go down while you are still angry."

 *Pretty Little* CHALLENGE ~ Don't let anger get the

best of you. You have two choices: Give God control or

give anger control. Give God control of your anger and He

will help you manage it.

MISSING OUT

Have you ever felt like you were missing out? I know it is not a good feeling when you think that you are missing out on something. Sometimes when we get saved at a younger age, we can feel like we are missing out on what other people call 'rites of passage'.

When you dedicate your life to Christ, you are not missing out. What the world offers cannot compare to what God gives. Living a set apart life is not a waste of time and is not done in vain.

Temporal things will not sustain you. The world can't outdo God. God is all that you need in every situation. The devil will try to make you think that living for the world is glamorous and fun, but it is all a charade. It is a crumbling lie that we should see for what it is.

Matthew 6:33 "But seek first his kingdom and his righteousness, and all these things will be given to you as well."

Pretty LittleCHALLENGE ~ Seek after God and the things of God rather than the things of this world.

It will pay off!

Pretty Little

STUDY TIPS

STUDY TIPS

Young women ask me all the time how to study the Word of God. Here are a few tips that I use personally to help me study the Bible. We are to study to show ourselves approved. I hope that at least one of these tips can help you in your own devotional time with the Lord.

1. You have to prepare your heart:

    There are things that are in the Word of God that are beyond our understanding. We have to pray and ask God that He would reveal to our hearts what He is trying to convey to us.

    We have to clear our hearts of bitterness and hurt. A key scripture I quote over myself is found in Psalms 51. It says, *"Create in me a clean heart and renew in me a right spirit."*

    We have to be willing to let God operate on our hearts so that we may understand Him and His Word better.

2. We have to get our minds right:

    We absolutely have to get our minds right before we can truly get all that the Word has to offer. Not only do we need open hearts, we need an open minds. We can't always comprehend His goodness but we can believe in it. There is always a battle in your mind. There is a battle of good and evil. Clear your mind of doubt and fear. Get your mind on Jesus and off of your problem.

3. We have to prepare our spiritual eyes and ears:

We have to remove all distractions. We need to turn off the cell phone and turn off the TV. We need to prepare ourselves to receive. We can do this by ushering in His presence with thanksgiving and praise. Turn on some worship music and begin to worship Him. Talk to Him.

You may not see Him with your physical eyes but you can feel Him in the depths of your spirit. You will be able to hear His voice with your spiritual ears.

4. Push past feelings:

There will be times when you do not feel like reading the Bible. That is probably the time you need to get into it the most! We do not walk by feeling; we walk by faith. Push through the not wanting to, be persistent, and make your flesh get into the Word.

5. Make the time:

I know that most of us are very busy, but we should never be too busy for God. God is not too busy for us when we need Him. It is not about finding the time; it is about making the time. Make a time to study God's Word.

6. We have to be consistent:

Have you ever been really on fire and could not get enough of the Word and then other times you did not even feel like reading the shortest Psalm? I think we all have probably been there.

When we go back and forth between reading and not reading, our faith becomes like a roller coaster. Why? Because we were not consistent in the Word and not consistently building our faith.

Reading the Bible should be a habit in your life every single day of the week. They say that once you do something for so long, it becomes a habit. We need to start building holy habits in our lives.

7. Write your own devotionals:

It is great to read what other believers get out of scripture. But God can speak to your heart just like He speaks to mine.

The great thing about writing your own devotionals is that it is what God revealed to you. God will give you revelations on scripture that directly apply to your situation.

Write down what you get out of a scripture, ponder it, and meditate on it. Years from now you will be able to look back at what the Lord spoke directly to you. Another great thing is that it is more personal and when you write things down, you remember them better.

There are no right and wrong ways to write a personal devotional. Just write down what God placed on your heart about the scripture you have read.

Read a verse and write down notes. Read a verse and write what it means to you. Read a verse and write down how it applies to your situation. Read a verse and write down what you would like it to do in your life. Read a verse and write down how you can apply it.

Those are all ways that you can write your very own personal devotionals. It will mean more to you when God speaks it directly to your heart. When He speaks, write it down and make it plain.

8. Be accountable:

Have a friend hold you accountable when it comes to reading the Bible. Find a study buddy. Find someone who you can talk to about what you have read. Share and listen. Talk with each other about what the scripture has meant to you in your life.

How did it help you through? How did it encourage you? How did it motivate you?

If you know of someone who is going through something find a scripture to encourage them. Make it your mission to share the gospel. Hide the Word in your heart so it is there whenever you need it! Choose to be chosen! He is calling you higher! Depend on Him and He will show you the way.

2 Timothy 2:15 (KJV) "Study to shew thyself approved unto God, a workman that needeth not to be ashamed, rightly dividing the word of truth."

Psalm 119:105 "Your word is a lamp for my feet, a light on my path."

Psalm 119:11 "I have hidden your word in my heart that I might not sin against you."

Isaiah 40:8 "The grass withers and the flower fades, but the word of our God shall stand forever."

Get in the Word for yourself and let His Word shape you and mold you into the person you were always meant to be!

About the Author

Mandy Fender has served in youth ministry for over ten years and loves to see what God is doing in every generation. She lives in the great state of Texas with her family and mean-mugging bulldog, Ziggy Zoo.

To find out more go to:
mandyfender.com

Connect

 Mandy Fender Author Page

 @mandyfender11

More Books by Mandy Fender

Beautifully Broken
Mighty God Girls: devotionals for girls ages 7 to 11
The Defier Series